WEATHER

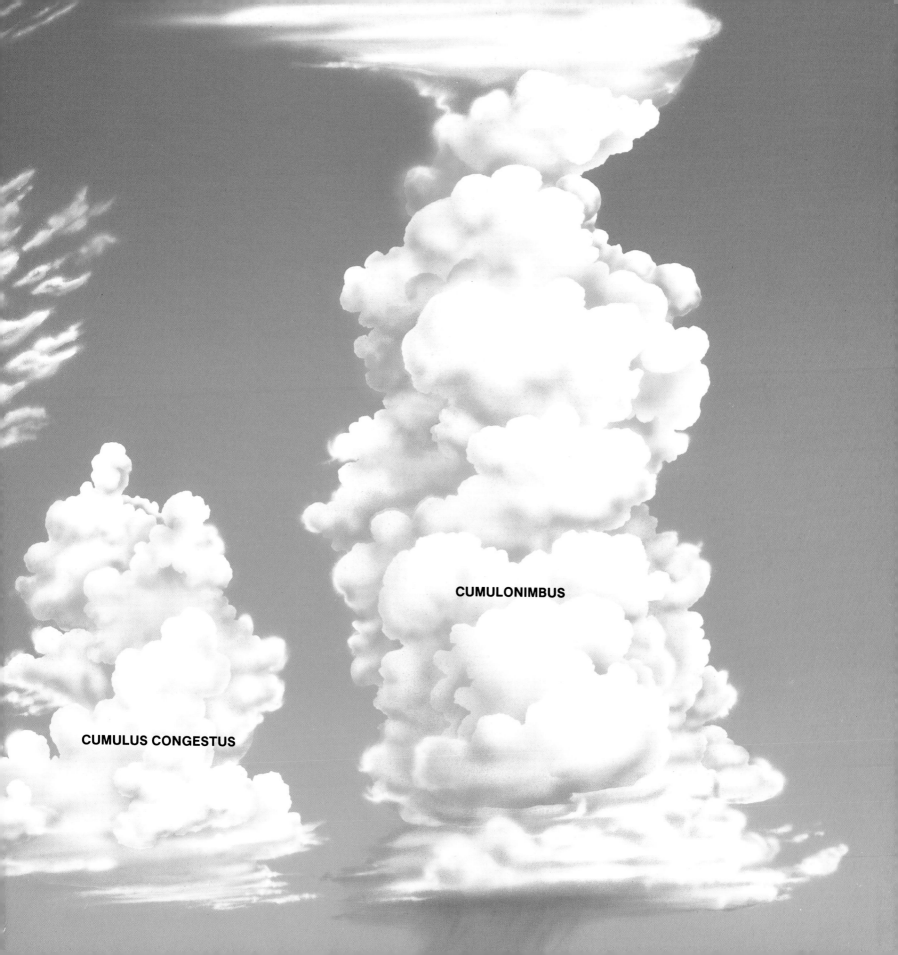

WEATHER

SEYMOUR SIMON

 Smithsonian |  Collins

An Imprint of HarperCollinsPublishers

"Nor'east to sou'west winds; . . . high and low barometer; . . .
probable areas of rain, snow, hail, and drought, succeeded
or preceded by earthquakes with thunder and lightning."

—Mark Twain on New England weather,
December 1876

"Everybody talks about the weather,
but nobody does anything about it."

—Charles Dudley Warner
in the *Hartford Courant,*
August 1897

PHOTO AND ART CREDITS

Photograph on page 17 courtesy NASA; photographs on pages 23, 24, 25, 29, and 31 courtesy National Center for Atmospheric Research; photograph on page 26 courtesy Skip Moody/Dembinsky Photo Associates; photograph on page 27 courtesy Virgil Haynes/Dembinsky Photo Associates; all other photographs by Seymour Simon. Artwork on pages 8, 9, 11, 14, and 15 and on endpapers by Ann Neumann.

The name of the Smithsonian, Smithsonian Institution and the sunburst logo
are registered trademarks of the Smithsonian Institution.
Collins is an imprint of HarperCollins Publishers.

Weather
Copyright © 1993 by Seymour Simon
Manufactured in China. All rights reserved.
No part of this book may be used or reproduced in any manner whatsoever without written permission except in the case of brief quotations embodied in critical articles and reviews. For information address HarperCollins Children's Books, a division of HarperCollins Publishers, 1350 Avenue of the Americas, New York, NY 10019.
www.harperchildrens.com
Library of Congress Cataloging-in-Publication Data
Simon, Seymour.
Weather / Seymour Simon.
p. cm.
Summary: Explores the causes, changing patterns, and forecasting of weather.
ISBN-10: 0-06-088440-1 (trade bdg.) — ISBN-13: 978-0-06-088440-6 (trade bdg.)
ISBN-10: 0-06-088439-8 (pbk.) — ISBN-13: 978-0-06-088439-0 (pbk.)
1. Weather—Juvenile literature. 2. Meteorology—Juvenile literature. [1. Weather. 2. Meteorology.] I. Title.
QC981.3.S56 1993   92-31069
551.5—dc20   CIP
                                                    AC
1 2 3 4 5 6 7 8 9 10
❖
Revised Edition

Smithsonian Mission Statement

For more than 160 years, the Smithsonian has remained true to its mission, "the increase and diffusion of knowledge." Today the Smithsonian is not only the world's largest provider of museum experiences supported by authoritative scholarship in science, history, and the arts but also an international leader in scientific research and exploration. The Smithsonian offers the world a picture of America, and America a picture of the world.

Natural History Mission Statement

We inspire curiosity, discovery, and learning about nature and culture through outstanding research, collections, exhibitions, and education.

It's cloudy today. It's also sunny, rainy, and snowy, hot and cold, calm and windy, dry and damp. Each of these descriptions of the weather is true every day of the year, someplace in the world.

We live in the atmosphere, the enormous ocean of air that surrounds Earth. Weather is what's happening at the bottom of the atmosphere, mostly in a layer seven and a half miles thick called the troposphere. (*Tropo* comes from a Greek word meaning "change.") Above the troposphere, another layer called the stratosphere extends up to about thirty miles. (*Strato* comes from a Greek word meaning "covering.")

Living in the troposphere, we feel the weather in the temperature of the air and the wetness of the rain. We see the weather in the puffy clouds and the white snow. We even hear the weather in the clatter of hail against a roof and the distant rumble of thunder.

Earth's weather is driven by the intense heat of the sun. The sun's energy travels through space in the form of visible light waves and invisible ultraviolet and infrared rays. About one third of the energy reaching Earth's atmosphere is reflected back into space. The remaining two thirds is absorbed during a process called insolation (from *in*coming *sol*ar radi*ation*).

The atmosphere lets sunlight pass through. Sunlight heats the ground, which in turn warms the air near the surface. But the atmosphere prevents most of the heat from escaping into space. This is called the greenhouse effect, because the glass windows in a greenhouse trap heat in the same way.

Insolation and the greenhouse effect strike a balance and make our planet livable. If Earth's average temperature were to drop by a few degrees, the ice ages would return and glaciers would cover North America and Europe. If the temperature were to increase by a few degrees, the polar ice caps would melt and the oceans would flood low-lying coastal lands.

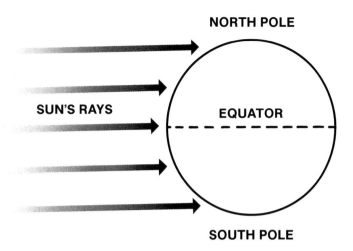

NORTH POLE

SUN'S RAYS   EQUATOR

SOUTH POLE

The sun doesn't warm Earth evenly. At the equator, where the sun's rays are most direct, insolation is several times greater than at either of the poles, where the sun's rays come in at a slant. Most of Earth's hot spots are located near the equator, and most of the cold spots are in the Arctic or Antarctic.

The unequal heating of Earth sets the atmosphere in motion. Air near the equator is heated, becomes lighter, and rises. At the poles, the colder air becomes heavier and settles downward. Warm equatorial air moves poleward while cold polar air moves toward the equator. The constant exchange of warm and cold air between equator and poles is one key to the giant atmospheric patterns that make up the weather.

But nothing about the weather is very simple. Earth spins rapidly from west to east. At the equator, the speed of rotation is about a thousand miles per hour, much faster than it is near the poles. The difference in speeds causes winds and ocean currents to curve to their right in the Northern Hemisphere and to their left in the Southern Hemisphere.

Earth's spin, its irregular surface features, and differing amounts of water in the air cause complex and variable wind patterns. These are called wind belts and have names such as the jet streams (narrow bands of high-speed upper atmospheric winds) and the trade winds (winds that blow east to west on both sides of the equator). Some regional winds also have colorful names, such as chinook (the warm wind that rushes down the eastern slopes of the Rocky Mountains), haboob (a North African dust storm), and sirocco (a Mediterranean wind that blows from the hot Sahara).

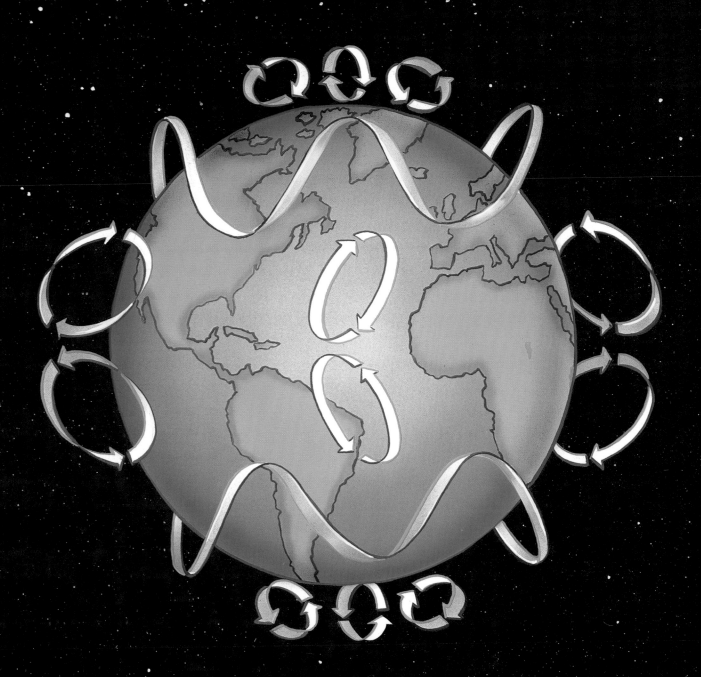

Many other things affect air temperature and weather conditions. For example, forests and trees absorb most of the sun's energy that falls on them, while a fresh snowfall reflects as much as nine tenths of the sun's energy. Mountaintops, such as these in the Olympic Mountains in Washington State, remain snow covered during summer months even while flowers bloom on the lower slopes. Mountains are cold because air temperatures drop about 3.5° Fahrenheit with each thousand feet of altitude. On high peaks, temperatures may be below freezing year round.

Water warms up and cools off much more slowly than land does. Oceans and other large bodies of water store heat from sunlight and release it slowly at night and during the winter. Land areas can't store much heat and become hot or cold more rapidly. That's why mid-continental regions have warmer summers and colder winters than do coastal areas.

Our changing weather is the result of a continuous battle between large bodies of air called air masses. Masses of cold air and masses of warm air push each other back and forth across the land. The boundary line between air masses is called a front. If a cold air mass advances as a warm air mass retreats, the boundary is called a cold front. If warm air advances against cold air, the boundary is called a warm front.

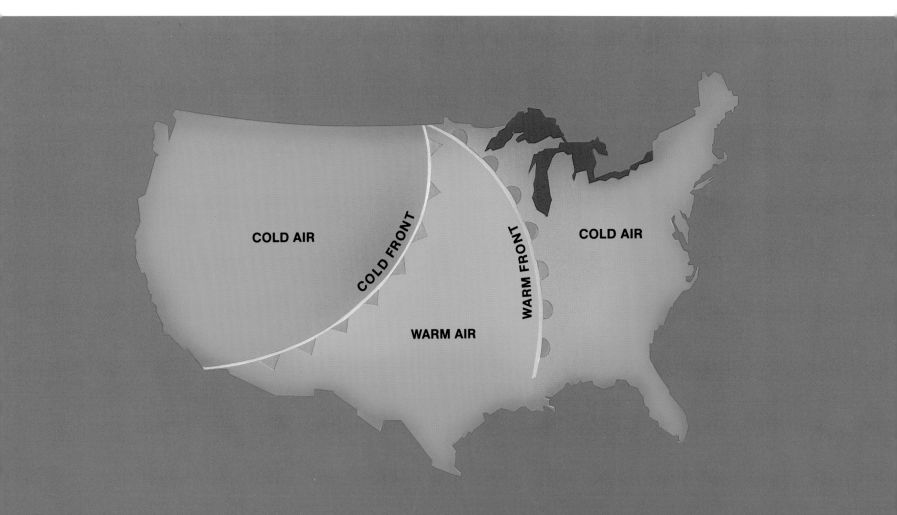

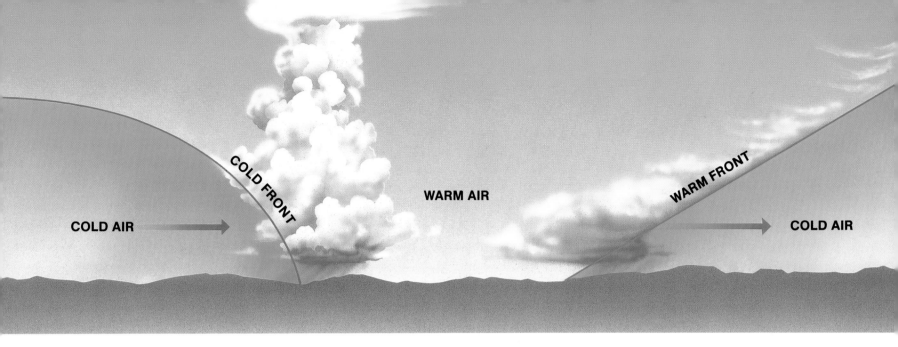

COLD FRONT

COLD AIR →

WARM AIR

WARM FRONT

COLD AIR

The weather of a region changes sharply every time a front and the air mass behind it pass over. Cold fronts move more rapidly than do warm fronts. When a cold front nears, the cold air forms a sort of a wedge and pushes the warm air aloft. Towering clouds form quickly and it may begin to rain or snow heavily. In a few hours, after the rain stops, the sky usually clears and the temperature drops.

Warm fronts arrive more gradually. Thin, high clouds build up a day or so in advance. As the front nears, rain or drizzle falls lightly and steadily. In winter, snow, sleet, or freezing rain may form as raindrops fall from the warm air into the cold air below.

Most of the water on our planet is in liquid or solid form. It is stored in oceans, lakes, ice caps, glaciers, rivers, or the ground. Only a small amount of water is in clouds, rain, snow, fog, frost, hail, or sleet, or is in the form of a gas called water vapor. Yet the tiny fraction of water that is in the air is more important than any other atmospheric substance in weather.

This view from a space shuttle shows clouds covering much of Earth's surface. Clouds may seem to be only white puffs or gray streaks, but if you begin looking at them more closely, they show a great variety of shapes and colors.

Scientists group clouds in families according to their shape and color. The three basic shapes of clouds are cumulus (meaning "mound"), stratus (meaning "spread out"), and cirrus (meaning "curly"). Other cloud words are nimbus (a rain cloud), cirro (high clouds), and alto (a mid-level cloud). When two names are combined, as in altostratus or cumulonimbus, the cloud has properties of both.

Cumulus clouds look like puffy, dome-shaped balls of cotton. These are low-level clouds, their bases less than a mile above Earth. Cumulus clouds are only a few hundred yards thick and are usually separated by patches of clear blue sky. They often form because of local heating during a sunny summer day and disappear in the cooler temperatures of evening.

Cumulus clouds sometimes build up into towering masses called cumulus congestus, or swelling cumulus, which may turn into cumulonimbus clouds. These often form in advance of a cold front where there are strongly rising air currents. At times, the tops of these clouds can reach six or seven miles above the ground, almost to the top of the troposphere. They are unstable clouds and rain showers frequently fall from them.

tratus clouds appear where there are no rising or falling air currents. These low-lying clouds form layers that are broad and thin, blanketing the sky and causing a gray day. When the clouds are thick enough, rain may fall. A stratus cloud that forms at ground level is called ground fog. It usually develops late at night or in the early morning. As the sun comes up, the heated ground makes the fog "burn off."

Cirrus clouds are thin, wispy, high-level clouds formed of ice crystals. Cirrus clouds often develop twenty to thirty hours before the arrival of a warm front and are a good forecaster of unsettled weather to come. Cirrostratus is another high-level cloud formed of ice crystals. These veil-like clouds are so thin that blue skies or bright stars often show through them.

Water that falls to the ground in liquid or solid form is called precipitation. The most common kinds are drizzle, rain, sleet, snow, and hail. Precipitation comes from water vapor in the air that has condensed to form clouds.

Clouds are made of tiny water droplets, ice crystals, or both. A cloud droplet is so small that the resistance of air prevents it from falling fast enough to reach the ground before it evaporates. For rain to fall, cloud droplets must grow thousands of times larger and much heavier. The mystery is how and why the tiny droplets come together to form large raindrops.

Scientists think that even in summer most rain begins as snow crystals. Snow crystals grow quickly and evaporate slowly, becoming heavy enough to fall. On the way down, they pass through warmer air, melt, and hit the ground as raindrops.

Snow begins in the same way as most rain. Snow crystals start to grow in the upper levels of towering cumulus clouds. Water vapor freezes directly onto the cold crystals. Finally, the crystals grow heavy enough to begin falling. If the air is cold all the way down, they reach the ground as snow. If the crystals melt on the way down and then refreeze as they pass through cold air, the frozen raindrops are called sleet.

A snowflake is usually six-sided, either a flat, plate-like shape or a long, columnlike form. Snow crystals are very complex, so no two snowflakes seem to be exactly alike, though they can be very similar

Hail forms in thunderstorms, usually during warmer weather. Hail begins as frozen raindrops that are tossed upward and downward by powerful gusts of air. Water freezes on the cold drops, and they become coated with layer after layer of ice. Finally, the pellets become too large to be held up by the winds, and they fall to the ground as hailstones.

Most hailstones are about the size of your little fingernail, but they can be the size of your fist. This photo of a large hailstone was taken in a special kind of light to show the different layers of ice crystals.

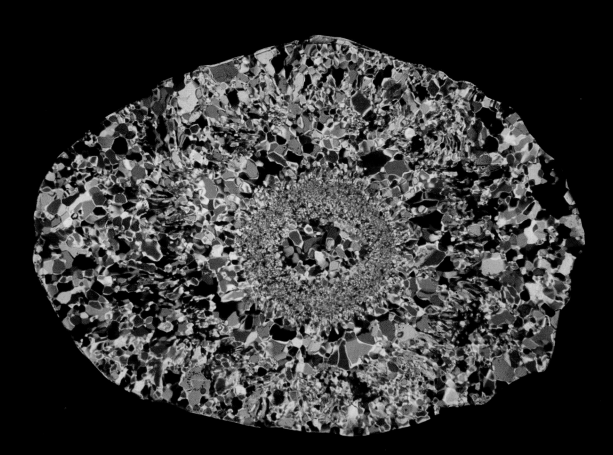

On clear, still nights, the ground, grass, shrubs, and other objects cool off very quickly. Sometimes they cool enough so that water vapor in the air condenses on them to form dew, in the same way that droplets of water collect on the outside of an icy pitcher on a hot summer day. Dew is not precipitation: it does not fall down from clouds but forms directly on cool surfaces, such as this spider web in the early morning.

Frost forms instead of dew if the temperature at which the moisture condenses is below the freezing point. On some cold winter nights, you may see feathery frost crystals form on the inside of your windowpane. Usually the heat from the morning sun quickly evaporates dew and frost.

Each year hundreds of thousands of weather balloons radio down information about atmospheric conditions. Here, a stratospheric weather balloon is inflated with helium, a lighter-than-air gas, before launch. These balloons can be up to eight hundred feet long and carry instrument payloads weighing more than two tons.

Every hour of the day and night, at weather stations around the world, instruments measure the weather. Thermometers show air temperature. Barometers show air pressure. Weather vanes and anemometers show wind direction and speed. Hygrometers measure humidity, and rain and snow gauges measure the amount of precipitation.

Hundreds of miles above Earth's surface, weather satellites beam down photos of cloud systems moving across the world. Meteorologists, scientists who study weather, use this information to learn about the weather and to forecast it.

Scientists cannot yet control the weather, but people's activities can change the weather, often not for the better. The photo shows a cumulus cloud forming above the smokestacks of a city. Older industrial cities that burn large amounts of coal and oil in factories and homes are often troubled by gray smog (a combination of the words "smoke" and "fog").

The smog typical of Los Angeles and Denver is caused mainly by the fumes from cars. This brown cloud forms near the ground and can reduce visibility and irritate the eyes, throat, and lungs. And both gray and brown smog can damage metal, rubber, and other materials.

Some scientists think that the greenhouse effect is increasing as a result of carbon dioxide released by huge forest fires in the tropics and the burning of fossil fuels in factories and automobiles. They say that Earth will warm by as much as 5° Fahrenheit in the next one hundred years, and that global heating will cause more powerful storms and other great changes in Earth's weather.

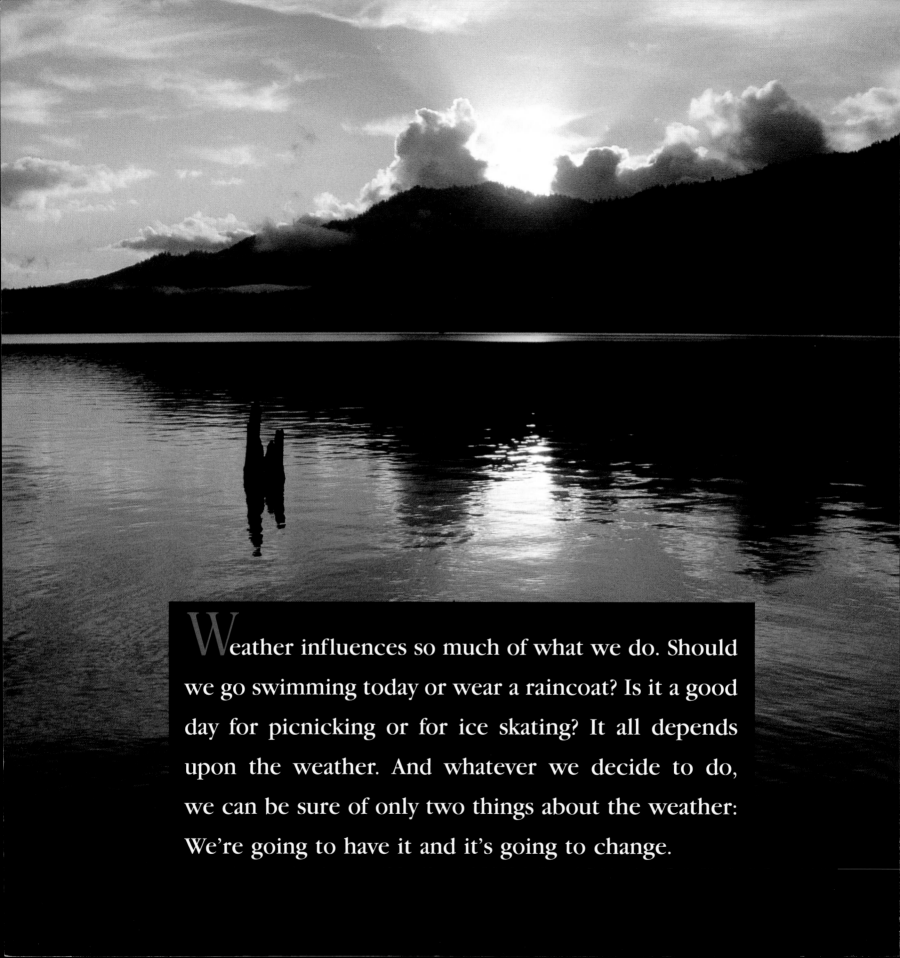

Weather influences so much of what we do. Should we go swimming today or wear a raincoat? Is it a good day for picnicking or for ice skating? It all depends upon the weather. And whatever we decide to do, we can be sure of only two things about the weather: We're going to have it and it's going to change.